DIARY OF A TRAINEE ROCK GOD

DIARY OF A TRAINEE ROCK GOD

JONATHAN MERES

With illustrations by

JAKE McDONALD

Barrington Stoke

First published in 2006 in Great Britain by
Barrington Stoke Ltd
18 Walker Street, Edinburgh, EH3 7LP

www.barringtonstoke.co.uk

This edition first published 2016

A CIP catalogue record for this book is available
from the British Library upon request

ISBN: 978-1-78112-600-4

Printed in China by Leo

Still for Noah

Saturday 15th October

Hi, and welcome to my diary. My name is Darren Smith. I'm almost 11 years old and I want to be a rock star. I *did* want to be a footballer, but I don't any more. I changed my mind when I met my new friend's big brother. He's called Nigel. What I mean is, my new friend's big brother is called Nigel, not my new friend. My new friend is called Steven.

Nigel is 14. He's got long hair and a guitar. I think he might have even got a girlfriend. Nigel wants to be a rock star too. He is *so* cool.

Nigel says there was this band called **Nirvana**. The singer was a guy called Kurt Cobain. And he kept a diary. Well, he didn't just *keep* a diary. He wrote in it as well! In the end, the diary got made into a book and loads of people bought it. Maybe my diary will get made into a book too. (So I'd better not swear, or write anything rude. Just in case my mum reads it!)

So anyway, we were all listening to **Nirvana**, in Nigel's room when Steven and Nigel's dad walked in. I thought he was going to tell Nigel to turn the music down, like mine would have done. But he didn't. He just stood there and then said, "'Smells Like Teen Spirit', eh? Great song!"

I couldn't believe it. Steven and Nigel's dad was really cool! But dads aren't supposed to be cool. Dads are boring. Well, my dad is. He wants me to call him Colin, by the way. Steven and Nigel's dad, I mean, not my dad. That would be stupid. My dad's called Trevor.

Colin went to see **Nirvana** playing live, in the last century. 1991 to be precise. They'd just released an album called *Nevermind*. It's got a picture of a bare naked baby swimming underwater, on the cover. (I'm not being rude, by the way, Mum. It really has!) I shouldn't think my dad's ever been to a rock concert in his life. But Colin's been to loads. He even met Steven and Nigel's mum at a concert! Except she wasn't their mum then. That would have been weird.

It was a concert by a band called **XTC**. This was like, way back in the 1980s or something. We're talking ancient history here! Anyway, Colin got talking to this girl. She was called Jane. They were both fans of the band. Their favourite song was a song called 'Making Plans For Nigel'. Well, one thing led to another and Colin and Jane ended up getting married. A few years later they had a baby. And guess what? They called him Nigel. Because 'Making Plans For Nigel' was like, their special song or something!

·How cool is that? Being named after a song! I wish I'd been named after a song. But there aren't any songs with Darren in the title. Not as far as I know, anyway.

5 songs with boys' names in the title

- **Michael** – FRANZ FERDINAND

- **Tony's Theme** – PIXIES

- **John, I'm Only Dancing** – DAVID BOWIE

- **Arnold Layne** – PINK FLOYD

- **Ben** – MICHAEL JACKSON

5 songs with girls' names in the title

- **Polly** – NIRVANA

- **Lola** – THE KINKS

- **Lucy In The Sky With Diamonds** – THE BEATLES

- **Come On Eileen** – DEXY'S MIDNIGHT RUNNERS

- **Virginia Plain** – ROXY MUSIC

Sunday 16th October

Just been round to Steven's house again. Nigel is such a wicked guitar player. His fingers were going up and down the guitar so fast, they were just a blur! Which is also the name of a band. **Blur**, I mean. Anyway I asked Nigel how long he'd been playing for. He said, "About 20 minutes." I said no, I mean when did you *first* start playing guitar. He said, "Three years ago."

Three years ago? That means Nigel must have started playing guitar when he was 11. And I'll be 11 next week! So if I start to play guitar now, maybe I'll be as good as Nigel when I'm his age. Wow! Just think!

There's just one teensy problem. I don't have a guitar.

But, hey, that's OK, because I don't think Mum and Dad have got me my birthday present yet. So maybe I should start dropping hints? It worked last year with the Man United strip and the FIFA game. But perhaps it's too late to drop hints. Perhaps I should just tell them.

You never know. It might work. Mind you, I bet I have to do something in return. It's always the same with my parents. Well, it's always the same with my dad anyway. He never just says, yes of course you can have a new pair of trainers, Darren. It's always, yes of course you can have a new pair of trainers, Darren. If you cut the grass, or tidy your room, or do the stupid washing-up for the next 18 years, or something.

But I don't mind. Not if it means I get an electric guitar for my birthday! Hey, if it means I get an electric guitar, I'll jump through a hoop of fire naked if I have to!

Steven's not very interested in rock music. He's much more into football. That's how we became friends in the first place. He'd only just moved to our school and we were both on the same team one lunch-time. He made a goal for me. I made one for him. That was it. We were best mates after that.

Football's all me and Steven ever seem to talk about. It's funny. I didn't even know he had a brother until I went to his house. He'd never said anything about him before. I don't think he knows just how cool Nigel is.

Anyway, guess what? Nigel let me have a go on his guitar. Not that I could play it or anything. But I held it! Nigel said I could strum it if I wanted, so I did. It sounded great. And dead loud. That's because it was plugged into an amp. 'Amp' is short for 'amplifier'.

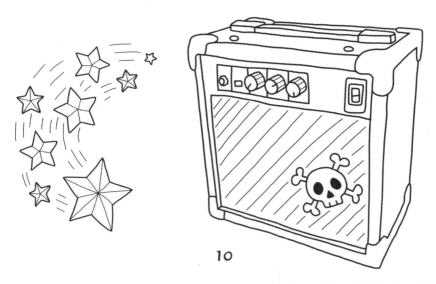

Nigel said that the long bit of the guitar is called the neck. The neck has lots of lines going across it. They're called frets. That's so that you know how far up the neck to put your fingers. At the end of the neck there are these things called tuning pegs. Some people call them machine heads. You turn them when you want to tune the strings and make them sound just right. There are six strings on Nigel's guitar, by the way, but some guitars have twelve strings. Oh, and under the strings there are these things called pick-ups. They make the guitar sound electric when you plug it into the amp.

Nigel showed me how to play something called a chord. That's when you play several notes together at the same time. You have to press down on a few of the strings in different places. Your fingers make a kind of shape. The chord I played was called D major. It felt a bit weird, but it sounded OK. Nigel said I was a natural. He said I'd be as good as Jimi Hendrix before I knew it! I bet Jimi Hendrix didn't only know one chord though. I bet he knew loads.

Nigel says that Jimi Hendrix was one of the best guitarists ever. And he didn't just play guitar, he sang and wrote songs as well. He wrote loads of well-known songs like 'Purple Haze', 'Crosstown Traffic' and 'Voodoo Chile'. And guess what? He was so amazing, he could play guitar with his teeth! And behind his back!

Sometimes he even set fire to his guitar on stage. I don't understand that. If I ever get an electric guitar, the last thing I'm going to do is set fire to it!

Some more famous guitarists

- **Jimmy Page** – LED ZEPPELIN

- **Keith Richards** – THE ROLLING STONES

- **John Frusciante** – RED HOT CHILI PEPPERS

- **Slash** – GUNS 'N' ROSES & VELVET REVOLVER

- **The Edge** – U2

- **Eric Clapton**

- **Kirk Hammett** – METALLICA

- **Angus Young** – AC/DC

- **Carlos Santana**

- **Brian May** – QUEEN

- **Django Reinhardt**

- **Prince**

- **B. B. King**

Monday 17th October

Guess what? I did it! I told my parents what I wanted for my birthday. Mum was doing yoga. Dad was doing the crossword. I took a deep breath and came right out with it. "Guess what I want for my birthday? An electric guitar!"

Dad asked me what I wanted one of those for. So I told him that I was going to be a rock star.

"That's nice, dear," said Mum without moving a muscle. Well, apart from the muscles she needed to speak.

Dad didn't say anything else. Not just then. He just put the newspaper down and took a sip of coffee. I thought, here we go. Any second now he's going to start droning on about how there were no such things as electric guitars when he was a boy and how he was lucky if he got a bar of chocolate for his birthday. But he didn't. He just said he'd think about it. Which was better than saying no, I suppose.

By the way, there *were* such things as electric guitars when my dad was a boy. My dad's old, but he's not quite *that* old. In fact, electric guitars have been around since the 1940s. That's amazing. That's before my grandparents were born!

Oh and I know all about the history of the electric guitar now. I googled it. Loads of stuff came up. Some of it was great. Like all the different makes of guitar you can get and stuff.

Fender and Gibson are probably the most famous makes of electric guitars. They haven't changed all that much since they were first made.

Fender's not a made up word. There was a guy called Leo Fender who invented two types of electric guitar. One was called a Fender Telecaster and the other was called a Fender Stratocaster. Then there was a guy called Les Paul. He invented an electric guitar called the Gibson Les Paul. How cool is that? Having a guitar named after you? Maybe one day there'll be a type of guitar called the Darren Megacaster!

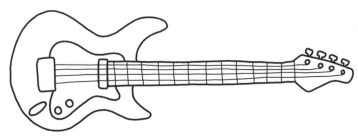

Anyway, after I'd been googling for a while, Dad called me downstairs again. He said that he'd had a think. I was like, come on then, Dad! Spit it out! Can I have an electric guitar or not? (I didn't say that of course. But I thought it.)

Dad didn't say anything for ages. It was like one of those talent shows on TV. You know, when the presenter says, "The person leaving the show tonight is ..." and then doesn't say anything for about an hour. It drives you mad! Well, it drives *me* mad anyway.

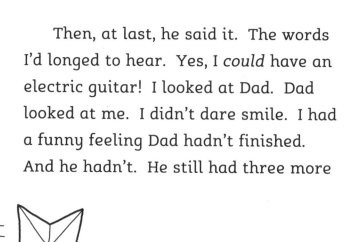

Then, at last, he said it. The words I'd longed to hear. Yes, I *could* have an electric guitar! I looked at Dad. Dad looked at me. I didn't dare smile. I had a funny feeling Dad hadn't finished. And he hadn't. He still had three more

words to say. Three more words I *hadn't* longed to hear.

"On one condition."

AAAAAAAAGGGGHHHH!!!

I told you, didn't I? Why does there always have to be a condition? Why do I always have to do something first? But again, I didn't say that. I just thought it.

"And what is that condition, Darren?" I hear you ask. Well, I'll tell you. Between now and my birthday, Dad's going to give me three clues. And if I can work out what those clues mean, I get an electric guitar!

That's the bad news.

The *good* news is that the clues are all going to have something to do with rock music. Which is brilliant, because I can just look stuff up on the internet! And if it's not on the internet? I'll just ask Nigel. Nigel knows everything there is to know about rock!

My top 10 guitar brands

1. Fender

2. Gibson

3. Epiphone

4. Gretsch

5. Ibanez

6. Rickenbacker

7. Vintage

8. Squier

9. Stagg

10. B. C. Rich

Tuesday 18th October

Dad gave me my first clue today. He wrote it on a bit of paper and put it on the kitchen table. It was there waiting for me when I went down to breakfast.

"A singer in a well-known rock band who sounds like a city in the north of England."

I looked at the clue for ages. I didn't know where to start. There are so many different rock bands. And so many cities. And anyway I'm rubbish at crossword clues. It's all right for Dad.

He does his stupid crossword every day. I never do crosswords. I'm rubbish at them!

I began to think that maybe getting my guitar wasn't going to be that easy after all. My dream of becoming a rock star was fading fast. I'd be lucky to get an electric guitar for my 12th birthday, never mind my 11th.

Just then there was a knock at the door. It was Steven. He'd come round to see if I fancied a kick-about. There's no school at the moment because it's half-term.

I was really glad to see Steven, even if I don't like football any more. Well, I mean I *do* like football. Just not quite as much as I used to. But I didn't say anything. I didn't want to upset Steven. And anyway football would give me something else to think about. You know, instead of working out stupid clues and stuff.

So, we played football for a while and it was great. I was Man United. Steven was Chelsea. Chelsea won 37–21. But I didn't care.

Then Steven asked me if I wanted to go round to his house. I asked him if Nigel would be there. Steven said yes he would. So I said OK, in that case I'd go round. Steven gave me this look. I think I might have upset him after all. I didn't mean to, but I think I did.

As soon as we walked through the front door I could hear music coming from Nigel's room. It was hard to describe. The music I mean, not Nigel's room. Nigel's room is easy to describe. It's dead cool. The walls are covered in posters of bands and rock stars and stuff.

There's a poster of David Bowie and there's one of Kurt Cobain. And there's one of this band called **The Arctic Monkeys**. They come from Sheffield. Which is a city in the north of England. But the singer is called Alex Turner, not Alex Sheffield! So that wasn't the answer to the clue.

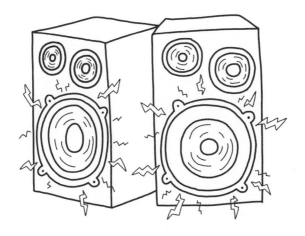

The music I could hear coming from Nigel's room had loud bits and soft bits, like **Nirvana**'s music does. But the singer sounded nothing like Kurt Cobain. Kurt Cobain had a gritty sort of voice.

Like he gargled with a bucket full of gravel every morning or something. The guy singing this music had a much smoother kind of voice. And he could sing really high. It was like he was a grown-up choir boy or something.

When Nigel came down, I asked him what the name of the band was. He said they were called **Radiohead** and that the album was called *OK Computer*. I said, that's a cool name for an album. Nigel said I should check them out, because they'd recorded lots of other albums as well, like *The Bends* and *In Rainbows*.

So anyway when I got home I listened to loads of **Radiohead** songs on YouTube. Songs like 'Karma Police', 'No Surprises' and 'Fake Plastic Trees'. But my favourite was this really mad song called 'Paranoid Android'. It was

dead long and complicated. Well,
it sounded complicated to me.

Anyway, I started googling and
finding out all about the band and stuff.
And guess what? The singer of **Radiohead**
is called Thom Yorke.

Thom Yorke! Do you get it?

**"A singer in a well-known rock band who
sounds like a city in the north of England ..."**

Well, York is a city in the north of England.
OK, so it's not spelled quite the same. But Thom
Yorke *sounds* like a city in the north of England!

I rushed downstairs and told Dad. He said,
"Is that your final answer?" You know, like they
do on quizzes on the TV? So I said yeah. Then

he said, "Do you want to phone a friend?" I said no. So then he looked at me and did one of those great big long pauses. Then guess what? He said I was right.

Yeah! Rock stardom here I come!

Some more stuff about Radiohead

- They got together in Oxford in 1986. They used to be called 'On A Friday' because that's the day that they practised.

- There are two brothers in **Radiohead**. Their names are Colin and Jonny Greenwood.

- The full line-up is

    Thom Yorke – VOCALS AND GUITAR
    Jonny Greenwood – GUITAR
    Ed O'Brien – GUITAR
    Colin Greenwood – BASS
    Phil Selway – DRUMS

- One of Thom Yorke's best friends is Michael Stipe. Michael Stipe was the singer in a band called **R.E.M.** (But **R.E.M.** weren't from Oxford. They were from Athens. Not Athens in Greece. Athens in the USA.)

○ Jonny Greenwood and Phil Selway both appeared in *Harry Potter and the Goblet of Fire*. Not the book. The film! How cool is that?

Wednesday 19th October

When I came down to breakfast this morning the next clue was already waiting for me.

"Could this charming band from Manchester be distant cousins?"

I read the clue over and over again. But I still didn't get it. What on earth was Dad on about now? This charming band? Distant cousins? From Manchester? We don't have any cousins in Manchester. I wish we did, because then we could visit them and I could go and watch Man United!

After a while, Dad came and sat down next to me. He asked how I was getting on with clue number two. I told him that I wasn't getting on at all. Big mistake! Dad started going on and on about not giving up and how you've got to keep on trying if you really want to ... *blah blah blah*.

Talk about boring! But the thing is, I kind of knew Dad was right. Deep down I knew that I couldn't give up and that I've got to keep on trying. It's the only way I'm ever going to get an electric guitar for my birthday!

There was only one thing for it. It was time to go and see Nigel again.

When I got round to the house, Steven came to the door. He didn't seem very happy to see me. Mind you, I don't blame him. I think he knew I was only there to see Nigel.

Then his dad, Colin, appeared. He said, "Nigel tells me you're into **Radiohead**, Darren. Great band. Saw them at Glastonbury in 2003. They were amazing."

I had no idea what Glastonbury was, so Colin told me. He said it was a huge music festival that's held every year on a farm in Somerset, which is in south-west England. It's on for three days and you get to see millions of bands! In 2003 Colin saw **R.E.M.**, **Manic Street Preachers**, **Echo and the Bunnymen** and a band from Iceland, called **Sigur Rós**. As well as **Radiohead** of course. It sounds brilliant! And guess what? Next year he's going to take Nigel.

Some news just in!

Colin is the Coolest Dad in the World! (Not like some dads I know.)

I went upstairs and
knocked on Nigel's door.
Nigel shouted for me to
come in, so I did. He was
lying on the floor, listening to music and flicking
through a great big pile of magazines. The
magazines were all about music and bands and
stuff. There must have been at least a hundred of
them. They looked great.

Nigel said that quite often you get a free
compilation CD with a music magazine. A
compilation is, like, loads of different tracks
by loads of different bands. I asked Nigel if he
knew any bands from Manchester. Without
even thinking, he said that **Oasis** were from
Manchester. (See? I told you Nigel knows
everything about rock, didn't I?)

Oasis had two brothers in them as well. Just like **Radiohead**. Their names were Noel and Liam Gallagher. Noel was the eldest. He played guitar and wrote the songs. Liam was the youngest. He was the main singer and played the tambourine. I think even I could play the tambourine! Yeah, and I might *have* to if I don't hurry up and solve these clues. Because I won't be getting an electric guitar at this rate, will I?

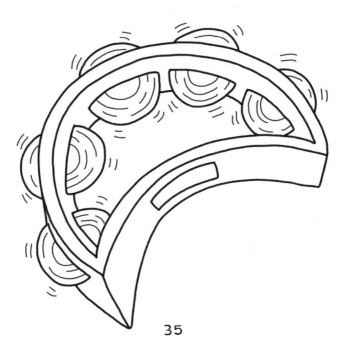

One of Nigel's magazines had a picture of the Gallagher brothers on the cover. I tried to think if they looked like anyone in our family, but they definitely didn't. They had dark hair and bushy eyebrows that met in the middle. There's no one in our family who looks like that! And the clue said something about being cousins.

I asked Nigel if he knew any more bands from Manchester. He told me to hang on and started looking at the magazines again. After

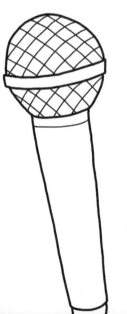

a few minutes he found one with a band called **The Stone Roses** on the cover. Nigel said they were really popular in the late 1980s and early '90s. The magazine had loads of stuff in it about other old bands from Manchester. They had names like the **Happy Mondays**, **Inspiral Carpets**, **James** and **New Order**. And guess what? They didn't call it Manchester, they called it *Mad*chester! I know. Weird or what?

Anyway, just before I left, Nigel gave me one of the compilation CDs. Not to borrow. To keep! He said it didn't matter because he'd got millions of them. I was dead pleased. But not as pleased as I was when I got home and looked at it.

Guess what one of the tracks was called? It was called 'This Charming Man'. And guess what the name of the band was? They were called **The Smiths**. And what's my name?

Darren Smith!

Do you see?

"Could this charming band from Manchester be distant cousins?"

It could only be **The Smiths**! I didn't know for sure that they were from Manchester. But two minutes and a quick google later, I did.

Two clues down – one to go!

Some stuff about The Smiths

- **The Smiths** formed in 1982 and split up in 1987.

- Their line-up was

  Morrissey – VOCALS
  Johnny Marr – GUITAR
  Andy Rourke – BASS
  Mike Joyce – DRUMS

- Morrissey sometimes appeared on stage wearing a fake hearing aid and waving a bunch of flowers around his head!

- J. K. Rowling is a big fan of **The Smiths**. (Hey, maybe that's why Harry Potter wears glasses?)

- Songs by **The Smiths** often have very long titles, like 'Heaven Knows I'm Miserable Now' and 'Last Night I Dreamt That Somebody Loved Me'. (That's two different songs by the way, not just one *really* long one.)

- Morrissey is a well-known vegetarian. One of **The Smiths** albums is even called *Meat Is Murder*!

- (Paul McCartney from **The Beatles** is another famous veggie rock star. His first wife, Linda, started the Linda McCartney range of vegetarian foods. I hope I don't get into trouble for advertising, but her veggie sausages are great!)

Thursday 20th October

Had this really weird dream last night. I dreamed that I was on stage, playing electric guitar in front of thousands and thousands of people! It was fantastic. But guess what? I could only play one chord. D major! It was like my fingers were stuck onto the neck of the guitar with superglue or something.

Yeah and things got even more weird when I woke up and went downstairs. Because the last clue was there, waiting for me, on the table. And this is what it said ...

 **"Never a cross word from this old punk? Try looking closer to home!"**

I must admit, I thought Dad had lost the plot completely. That's if Dad ever had the plot to begin with of course. Ha ha!

Anyway, Mum came over and sat next to me. She must have seen that I was looking a bit puzzled. I showed her the clue. When she read it she just grinned. I knew she knew the answer. But I also knew that she wasn't going to tell me what it was. I begged her to, but it was no good. Mum said that I had to solve the clue myself. She said that Dad would go up the wall if she helped me. I said yeah, that's because Dad's boring.

Mum just looked at me and said that maybe Dad wasn't *quite* as boring as I thought he was.

I said, "Oh yeah, why's that then?"

But all Mum said was, "Look in the loft."

Well, I didn't need to be told twice. I was back up those stairs like a shot! I got the long pole with the hook on the end and pulled open the loft trapdoor. Then I pulled down the metal ladder to get into the loft.

I felt dead excited. I'd never been allowed in the loft by myself before. It was dark and musty and a bit smelly. I felt around for the light switch and switched it on.

There, bang in the middle of the loft, was an old cardboard box. It was as if it had been put there on purpose. I went over to the box and looked at it. There was a sticker on top. It just said one word.

Punk!

I opened the box. It was full of old vinyl records. I took one out and looked at the cover. It was called ... Actually I'd better not say what it was called, because there was a rude word in the title. But it was by a band called **The Sex Pistols** (and, by the way, it's OK to say that word because that's a proper word and not a swear word or anything). The songs were called things like 'Pretty Vacant', 'Anarchy in the UK' and 'God Save the Queen'. And the singer was a guy called Johnny Rotten.

Oh and guess what? A name had been written on the back of the record in black felt pen. And what do you think the name was?

Trevor Smith!

I couldn't believe it. My dad was a punk rocker! Mum was right. Perhaps Dad's not quite as boring as I thought he was.

I took another record out from the box and looked at it. It was by a band called **The Clash**. There were four skinny guys on the cover, just staring at the camera and looking all mean and moody. I looked on the back. The singer was called Joe Strummer.

The next record I looked at was by a band called **The Damned**. One member of the band was called Rat Scabies and another one was called Captain Sensible! Then there was a record by a band called **Generation X**. Their singer was called Billy Idol!

It was starting to look like the first thing you needed to do, if you wanted to be in a punk band, was give yourself a silly name!

Then I found another record. It was by some band called **Des Troy and the Zits**. There was a picture of them. They all had spiky hair and were pulling stupid faces. One of them looked oddly familiar.

I looked more closely. I thought, 'Hang on, I know him.' And I did. In fact, I still do.

It was my dad!

Except he wasn't called Trevor Smith. He was Des Troy! Get it? Des Troy?

Destroy!

So not only was my dad a punk rocker, he was actually in a band too. A proper band! And they made a record and everything. It was incredible! And then I thought, 'Yeah that's the clue. The last clue! I've worked it out.'

**"Never a cross word from this old punk?
Try looking closer to home!"**

Some news just in! Steven and Nigel's dad is the *Second* Coolest Dad in the World!

My dad is the first!

Friday 21st October

Hi. Sorry I didn't do a list, or a fact file or anything yesterday. That's because I was in a state of shock. And I'm sorry but you won't be getting one today either. Want to know why? It's my birthday. And guess what I got?

An electric guitar!

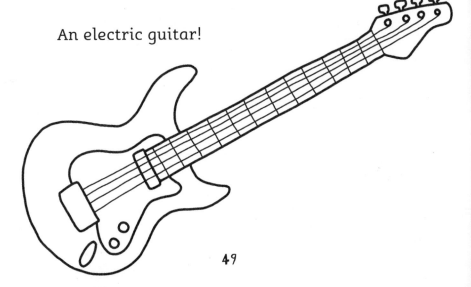

It's a beauty! It's black and white and it's a Fender Stratocaster. Well, not a *real* Fender. That would cost a small fortune. But it's *like* a Stratocaster. It's called a copy. Anyway, it's fantastic and I love it to bits! It came with an amp and everything. Now all I've got to do is learn to play it ...

Dad's going to show me a couple more chords. He says he only knows a few. He says you didn't

need to know many chords to play in a punk band! I told him about Nigel and how amazing he is on guitar. Dad said he'd love to hear him play one day.

Hey, that's an idea! Maybe I'll ask Nigel to come round some time.

If I get good at playing guitar we can form a band together. Yeah! And Steven can be the singer if he wants. I wonder what we could call ourselves?

I'd better start making a list!

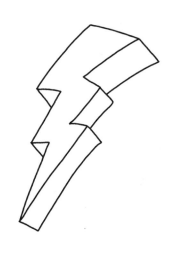

If you enjoyed this brilliantly
funny story, then you'll love ...

DANCING DEANO SHOWN RED CARD

Wonder kid footballer Dean has just moved into
George's village. George is football mad and soon she
gets to meet Dean. But Dean is always in trouble for
his antics. The papers reckon he's too rude, too rich
and too big for his golden boots – but can you always
believe what you read in the papers?